MYSTE
OF THE ANCIENT WORLD

IN SEARCH OF
KING MINOS

LOUISE STEEL

WEIDENFELD & NICOLSON

LONDON

The earliest civilization in Europe flourished on the island of Crete in the first part of the 2nd century BC. Of the many sites where remains of this civilization have been found, the most important is surely that at Knossos, on the north coast near to modern Herakleion, where a magnificent palace building has been excavated, a complete understanding of which eludes scholars to this day.

Porticoed vestibule by the north entrance to the palace of Knossos.

*S*ir Arthur Evans, the excavator of the palace of Knossos, in his workroom, c.1925.

Arthur Evans and the Discovery of Knossos

The story of the discovery of the fabulous palace at Knossos begins in Victorian England with the privileged upbringing of Sir Arthur Evans (1851–1941). The son of the renowned scholar, gentleman and antiquarian John Evans,

Evans grew up surrounded by the fine collections of Nash Mills manor house. The nineteenth century was a time of increasing interest in our ancestors and the young Arthur was raised in a family very much associated with the novel discipline of prehistory. As a young man Evans studied at Oxford University and subsequently travelled widely around the Balkans where he worked as a freelance journalist writing mainly for the *Manchester Guardian*. Evans's interest in the pre-Classical past of Greece and disappointment in what he saw as too great an emphasis on the splendours of the Classical world is evident very early on, but it was not until his appointment as the Keeper of the Ashmolean Museum in Oxford in 1884 that he had a chance to indulge his passion for prehistory. Evans's ambition at the Ashmolean was to assemble a new collection that would reflect a broad spectrum of archaeology but concentrate particularly on the prehistoric past.

In the 1870s the German entrepreneur Heinrich Schliemann, a friend of Evans's father, began explorations at Troy and on the Greek mainland, in search of the Trojan War of legend, and discovered a pre-Classical civilization of untold wealth. Evans was greatly impressed by Schliemann's discoveries in Greece, especially the fantastic wealth of the shaft graves where the early kings of Mycenae were buried. His sister Joan wrote, 'Arthur found his gold work from Mycenae beautiful, exciting and puzzling: it was an art which appealed to him, because it was not classical'; but while Schliemann had used these finds as illustrations of Homeric epic Evans saw their real potential as evidence of an important Bronze Age civilization in the Aegean. Gradually his attention turned to the island of Crete, specifically to the site of Knossos, which had already been identified as a suitable possibility for excavation by Schliemann. But it was not until 1900 that Evans could begin his excavations at the site, with the help of an experienced archaeologist, Duncan Mackenzie, the son of a Scottish gamekeeper.

At Knossos Evans uncovered the remains of a prosperous prehistoric

A **Black Figure
vase from
Athens (540–30 BC)
showing Theseus
killing the minotaur.**

civilization. This he named 'Minoan' after the legendary king Minos, who according to Greek legend demanded seven young men and seven young women from Athens as a sacrifice to the bull-headed monster, the Minotaur, who lived in a labyrinth below his palace. Dominating the Bronze Age town at Knossos was a large palace with a suitably complex ground-plan recalling the legend of Theseus and the Minotaur. Although Evans excavated at Knossos over many years, the greater part of the palace and its environs was actually excavated during the first five seasons. Alongside his excavations Evans engaged in an ambitious programme of restoration and rebuilt much of the palace structure in concrete. These 'restorations' are still visible today, dominating the site, and have a profound effect on the visitors' perception of ancient Knossos.

The Minoan Civilization

The Minoan civilization flourished on Crete during the earlier part of the 2nd millennium BC and is the earliest urban culture known in Europe. Minoan Crete was very wealthy and cosmopolitan, and had extensive trading and diplomatic links throughout the Aegean and with the Near East, especially Egypt. Crete is particularly well known for its imposing palaces, probably the residences of the local rulers. At least four such palaces have been excavated, at Phaistos, Mallia, Zakros and, most importantly, at Knossos. In addition to the palaces there were prosperous large towns, for example Palaikastro, Gournia

*G**igantic stone 'horns-of-consecration', or
stylized bull's horns, adorned the palace.*

***P**ainted relief
of a bull
from the north
entrance vestibule*

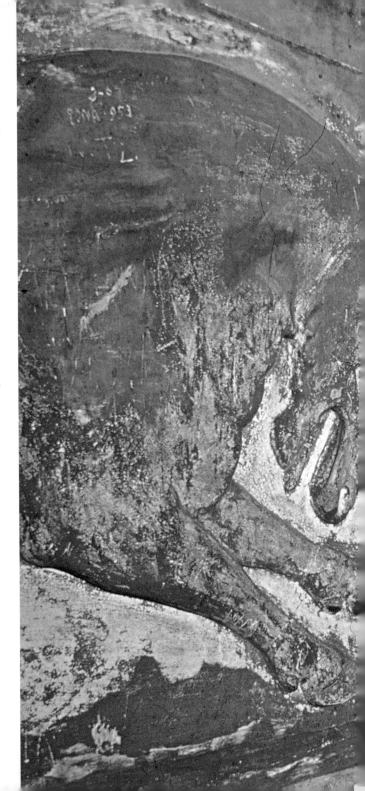

and Kommos, and several country houses or villas – miniature versions of the palaces, such as those at Amnisos and Ayia Triadha. Unfortunately for archaeologists the Minoan civilization is essentially prehistoric: although the Minoans were literate and used two different writing systems – hieroglyphs (not the same as Egyptian hierolglyphs) in the earlier palaces, and a form of writing known as Linear A in the later palaces – these were mainly used to record economic transactions on clay tablets, but the texts have never been deciphered and the language remains unknown.

The inhabitants of Minoan Crete enjoyed a high standard of living, which is particularly evident in the sophistication of the sanitation system in the towns. The prosperity of the island is reflected by the profusion of luxury items that have been recovered from the sites and the information that can be gleaned from the frescoes that adorned the palace walls. Minoan arts and crafts were renowned throughout the ancient world and were exported to Egypt, the Near East and within the Aegean. Minoans bringing gifts to the pharaohs are commonly painted on the tombs of the Egyptian nobles at Thebes, and many of the objects Schliemann found in the shaft graves at Mycenae were probably of Cretan craftsmanship. Other particularly noteworthy pieces are the famous steatite (soapstone) bull's head vase from Knossos, and the exquisite rock crystal *rhyton* (ritual vase) from Zakros. Other important Minoan art forms include seal engraving on semi-precious stones, such as carnelian; fine gold jewellery,

Minoan palace craftsmen were renowned throughout the ancient world, and their finely crafted stone and metal vases were highly valued throughout the East Mediterranean. A typical example is this fine bull's head rhyton made of steatite, a ceremonial vase associated with cult.

*F*aience statuette
of a snake goddess
from Knossos.

*S*ome of the finest
examples of wall
paintings in the Aegean
world are from the island
of Thera, possibly a Minoan
colony. Here the wealthy
citizens of the town
decorated their walls in
imitation of the elaborate
wall paintings from the
palace of Knossos. This
example shows a priestess
burning incense to an
unknown deity.

15

*D*etail of griffin from the Throne Room at Knossos.

especially seal-rings; and faience work, a form of glass paste used to make a variety of objects, such as the renowned statuettes of the snake goddess.

But the masterpieces of Minoan art are surely the colourful wall paintings that decorated the Minoan palaces. Several different types can be identified: impressionistic miniature scenes, usually ritual in character; larger formalized scenes of human figures; nature scenes; and general abstract motifs. Recent discoveries of apparently Minoan-style wall paintings in Egypt and the southern Levant suggest that this art form was quite widely disseminated around the large cosmopolitan palaces of the East Mediterranean as part of a common aristocratic style, perhaps the work of itinerant Minoan craftsmen.

Knossos

Knossos is the oldest inhabited site on the island of Crete and was occupied from the 7th century BC. The first settlers at Knossos were simple Neolithic farmers. For their settlement they chose a low hill close to the Kairatos stream and sufficiently inland to protect them from unwanted attention from the sea. Its central location on the north coast of the island, allowing easy communication by land with the rest of the island, was to prove very important to the development of Knossos and its cultural, political and economic pre-eminence during the Bronze Age.

View of the palace at Knossos.

The Palace at Knossos

Around 1900 BC a momentous change in Cretan society is reflected by the sudden appearance on the island of palaces – monumental buildings sharing a common plan and architectural features. This change was the sudden transformation of the simple farming communities of Crete into a fully fledged urbanized state (or states) with diplomatic and trading links with the east Mediterranean. The largest and most important of the palaces is at Knossos and it has a very long history. Around 1780 BC the palace was destroyed by an earthquake and the rulers at Knossos took this opportunity dramatically to

*T*he complicated ground-plan
of the palace of Knossos
recalls the ancient Greek myth of
Theseus and the Minotaur – a
monster with a man's body and
bull's head, which lived in the
labyrinth beneath the palace of the
Cretan king Minos. Scenes from a
Roman mosaic recounting this
myth – showing Thesesus and the
Minotaur, Ariadne giving the
thread to Theseus, the return of
the Athenian ships from Crete
and the design of the floor as a
labyrinth.

restructure the palace, incorporating various architectural innovations, but the basic architectural design, and presumably also the function of the palace, remained the same.

The plan of the palace of Knossos is very complicated, but in effect comprises a series of rooms of varying sizes and with varying functions, grouped around a large rectangular central court. The ground floor functioned as the palace basement, and was mainly used for storage and for workrooms. The main reception and residential rooms were located on the upper storeys of the palace, looking down on to the central court. The palace was not conceived of as a single unit planned on a single occasion, but instead is a classic example of agglomerative architecture, added to on many separate occasions. Because of the great length of time that the palace was in use there are many superimposed layers, and as a consequence the architectural history of the palace is very confusing.

The palace is approached by a number of impressive access routes, for example the well-paved royal road from the west, which passes through the town of Knossos. Immediately in front of the palace is the west court, a large paved area crossed by raised walkways. This is where the enclosed, private world of the palace came into contact with the open, public world beyond. The beautiful west façade of the palace is faced with large squared blocks of gypsum, which would have glistened in the bright sunlight and were designed to impress those who were not admitted to its interior and the various diplomatic and trading envoys who visited the ruler of Knossos.

The three large pits sunk into the west court were probably large granaries. Indeed, one of the most important functions of the palaces was the storage of vast quantities of agricultural produce that constituted tax payments. This, in turn, was used to support the vast army of craftsmen sponsored by the palace, who made the exquisite luxury objects so coveted by the rulers of Crete and central to her overseas trade.

The theatral area to the north-west of the palace is a paved square in front of a wide flight of shallow steps where spectators could gather. This was probably a communal place of assembly used for public ceremonies, to receive visitors who were not to be admitted inside the palace itself, or even to hear legal cases. The royal road leading from the town at Knossos ends just in front of the theatral area, implying that it was here where the townsfolk came into direct contact with the palace administration.

The main ceremonial entrance to the palace is on the west, through a long,

One of the main functions of the palace at Knossos was that of a massive central storage facility for large quantities of agricultural produce – grain and olive oil – which was stored in vast clay storage jars or **pithoi.**

narrow passageway, the corridor of the Procession Fresco. This was adorned with wall paintings showing men carrying elaborate luxuries, perhaps gifts or tribute for the ruler or offerings to a deity. Although idealized and influenced by Egyptian iconography, these wall paintings give us an idea of the ceremonial life of the court and were designed to impress visitors to the palace.

Architecturally, the focus of the palace was the central court, a large rectangular area which would originally have been paved. But the central court was very remote and access to it was restricted, suggesting it had a specific and probably ceremonial function. The rulers of Knossos would probably have supervised the activities in the central court, looking down on it from the main

A wall painting of the so-called priest king (left), at the end of the Procession Corridor, leading into the palace. Identified as a male member of the royal household by Evans, this wall painting in fact probably depicts a female, as is indicated by the pale skin. She is wearing a diadem – perhaps a Minoan symbol of office.

The ceremonial entrance into the palace of Knossos was through a narrow corridor (the Procession Corridor), the walls of which were richly adorned with wall paintings depicting men bearing valuable gifts to the ruler of Knossos (right).

*T*he so-called Throne Room is one of a series of small basement shrines which lined the eastern side of the central court of the palace at Knossos. The walls are brightly decorated with friezes of griffons, mythical animals of eastern origin, flanking a gypsum 'throne', possibly the seat of the presiding priest or priestess.

state rooms on the upper storeys. The north, south and east sides of this court would largely have presented a blank face, and the main activity of the central court lay within the series of small cult rooms that opened off its west side. Of these the most famous is undoubtedly the throne room. Evans originally believed that this room was the seat of the ruler of Knossos, but it is not the focal point of the palace and was probably a shrine. Against the side wall of the throne room there was a magnificent gypsum chair, flanked by griffins (a royal symbol adopted from the east); this might have been the seat of the goddess or of her human manifestation, the priestess.

Behind the suite of small cult rooms in the west there is a series of massive storerooms (magazines). Here the vast bulk of the agricultural produce (grain and olive oil) sent to the palace as taxes was kept in tall storage jars (*pithoi*). Scribes kept records of these transactions and their writing system was developed on clay tablets to administer the complicated palace bureaucracy.

The palace was largely independent from the neighbouring town of Knossos and to a certain extent resembled a microcosm of Minoan life, or a Minoan town in miniature. In addition to the many activities related to the administrative bureaucracy of the kingdom the palace also supported the numerous craftsmen engaged in the production of luxury wares, and their workrooms are mainly located in the north-east quarter of the palace.

*V*arious signs are incised on
the masonry of the palace –
possibly as mason marks?
Particularly common is the double
axe, such as this one on the wall of
the corridor connecting the storage
rooms.

*T*he Grand Staircase and
the doorway leading to the
royal apartments. The walls are
decorated with paintings of
'figure-of-eight' shields.

View of the royal apartments in the eastern area of the palace of Knossos. The most important rooms were above ground level.

The main reception and residential rooms, where the ruler and his family or the priests of Knossos lived, are located on the upper floor. These are best preserved in the east side of the palace. This warren of rooms on several floors were connected by the impressive stone-built grand staircase, of which four flights survive. The suites of rooms in the domestic quarter are essentially

*T*he palace was richly decorated with
fine wall paintings, such as this frieze
of naturalistic dolphins and fish which
adorned the walls of the queen's quarters in
the eastern sector of the palace.

A lustral basin in the northern part of the palace
— this sunken paved area was probably used
for ceremonial bathing or purification, perhaps
before entry into the palace.

isolated from each other to ensure maximum privacy, but are interconnected by cool dark passages. The rooms themselves are large and airy and are decorated with gaily coloured wall paintings, including the famous Dolphin Fresco.

Life for those residents of the palace who were members of the ruling class was very comfortable. Hygiene was an important concern, as was no doubt necessary in such crowded quarters, and there was a sophisticated sanitation system which included ample provision for bathing. Numerous lustral basins – interior sunken, stone-lined rooms probably used for bathing or ritual cleansing – are found throughout the palace. There was also a bathroom in the domestic quarter, where a clay bathtub was tucked away behind a low partition wall. Opposite the bathroom there is a lavatory, a small room housing a sophisticated flushing toilet. This comprises a toilet seat over a large drain which was connected to a perforated stone slab in the adjacent room. After the toilet was used water was poured down the hole in the stone slab, to flush the lavatory.

Function of the Palace

Although we known much about the internal organization of the palace, it is still not entirely clear what its actual role in Minoan society was. It certainly had a commanding position at the apex of Minoan society, and was responsible for the internal administration of the newly formed state and the integration of the Minoan world with the older civiliza-

tions of the Near East and Egypt on the levels of trade and diplomacy. Minoan palaces controlled the production and distribution of agricultural produce. The proceeds of this basic system served to support the manufacture of luxury objects for domestic consumption and for export. The importance of the administrative, economic and diplomatic roles of the palace and its predominance in Minoan society is reflected in its magnificent and imposing architectural façades.

We do not know who was at the apex of Minoan society, whether it was a largely secular king, or a more religious priest. Certainly the palace was the centre of ceremonial and religious activity, whose rituals and many other aspects of court life can be reconstructed from the wall paintings which adorned its walls. The miniature Grandstand Fresco depicts a large public gathering of the sort that might have taken place in the theatral area, the west court, or even in the central court. The dramatic bull-leaping scenes are powerfully evocative of the types of ceremonial, athletic events which might have

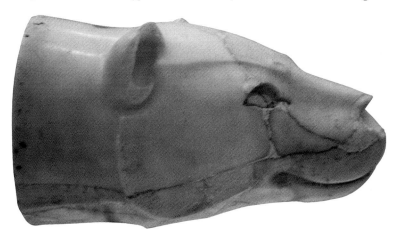

Wall painting from the Mycenaean palace of Tiryns, on the Greek mainland, depicting a woman in a procession, dressed in Minoan-style court dress.

Rhyton, or ceremonial vase, in the form of a lioness's head.

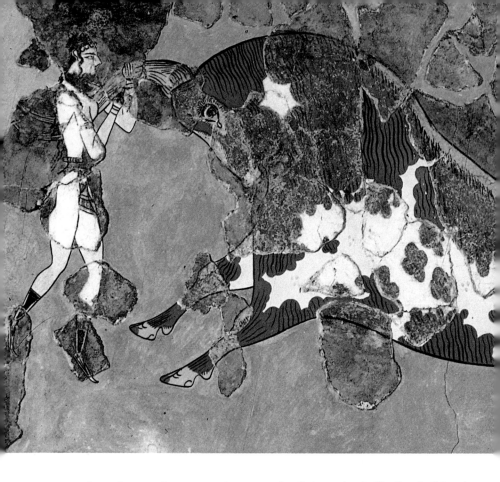

taken place as important elements of religious ritual. Similar bull-leaping scenes from Tell ed-Dab'a, in Egypt, suggest that this ceremony had a wider currency throughout the East Mediterranean at this time, or may have been an important Minoan import to Egypt along with the fine stone and metal vases depicted on Egyptian tombs.

As well as its important economic and ceremonial roles, the palace was also the home of the ruler of Knossos, his family and his followers. These individuals enjoyed a particularly luxurious lifestyle, surrounded by many comforts and shielded from the outside world by the imposing walls of the palace. The leisured life of these people is also depicted in the palace wall

*V**arious acrobatic games took place within the Minoan palace, perhaps part of a religious ceremony. This wall painting shows an acrobat leaping over a bull.*

paintings, especially the fine details of ladies' court dress and the drinking ceremonies of the Campstool Fresco.

While the palace at Knossos undoubtedly dominated Crete both physically and psychologically, being the heart of the Minoan powerbase, in many respects it remained a place of mystery and awe, with its central core remote and hidden from the outside world.

IN SEARCH
OF KING
MINOS

PHOTOGRAPHIC ACKNOWLEDGEMENTS
Cover AKG London; pp. 2–3, 4, 6–7, 8, AKG;
pp. 10–11 E.T. Archive [ETA]; pp. 13, 14, 15,
16–17, 18–19, 20–21, 23 AKG; pp. 24, 25, 26
ETA; pp. 28tl, 28–9 AKG; pp. 30–31 TRIP/B.
Turner; pp. 32–3 ETA; pp. 34–5, 36 AKG;
p. 37 TRIP/B. Turner; pp. 38–9 AKG.

First published in Great Britain 1997
by George Weidenfeld and Nicolson Ltd
The Orion Publishing Group
5 Upper St Martin's Lane
London WC2H 9EA

A CIP catalogue record for this book is available
from the British Library
ISBN 0 297 82273X

Picture Research: Joanne King

Designed by Harry Green

Typeset in Baskerville